Derby Old and New

by Frank Rodgers

*I felt a pleasure walking
around Derby* - James Boswell

Photographs and text by Frank Rodgers © 1996

ISBN 0 85100 125 4

Designed and published by
Derbyshire Countryside Ltd.,
Heritage House,
Lodge Lane, Derby DE1 3HE.
Telephone: (01332) 347087
Fax: (01332) 290688

Introduction

When *Derby Old and New* was first published in 1975 it had very good reviews, one describing it as 'a valuable historical document'. Very pleasing too were the letters which followed, especially those full of nostalgia from Derbians now living in Australia, New Zealand, America and other far away places. In the 21 years since it was first issued there have been many changes in the city, the most important, of course, being its elevation to that status in 1977.

Old maps show that the pattern of Derby's streets has changed little for over a century and towards the end of the 1960s it was no longer able to cope with the increasing flow of traffic. A new complex of roads crossing and recrossing the River Derwent on the east side of the town was constructed and opened in 1972, and this effectively diverts on to an inner by-pass much traffic which previously passed through the town centre. Systems of one-way traffic smoothed the flow through the old streets and pedestrian precincts enhanced by trees were created.

In the architectural changes there was opposition to the demolition of the railway station frontage in Midland Road and its replacement with what has been described as 'supermarket' architecture. The narrow streets around Eagle Street were swept away for the building of the Eagle Centre which also houses the stalls which stood in the Morledge. That area is now occupied by the Derby Combined Court Centre. These changes were recorded in the revised issues of 1985 and 1989.

This latest edition is in a new format, enlarged with all the 'new' photographs re-taken. Further pedestrianisation is recorded, notably the closure to traffic of St. Peter's Street and the Cornmarket, and the partial closure of St. Peter's Churchyard and St. James Street. The Market Place has been attractively paved and has a waterfall, the object of much adverse criticism, as too is the large stone figure of a ram in East Street.

In taking the 'new' photographs I found it increasingly difficult to stand on the same spot from which the original old photograph was taken, often caused by the planting of new trees; East Street presented a problem. I thank the City Library for their help and the loan of 'old' photographs, many by the well-known Richard Keen. The rest are from my own collection and a few postcards. Not all the 'old' photographs were dated, and by some research an approximation has been made. In all the three editions of *Derby Old and New* there was only one valid criticism from readers. This pointed out that the date given on an 'old' photograph was incorrect as a car shown had not yet been made at that time!

Frank Rodgers 1996

About the Author

Frank Rodgers was born at Weston Underwood in 1913 of an old Derbyshire farming family. Moving to Derby he grew to know the town well, resulting in his undertaking the compilation of *Derby Old and New* one of a series covering England, Scotland and Wales. This is the 4th revision, now published by Derbyshire Countryside Ltd. in a new format.

A keen photographer he has recorded many curious and fascinating features of the county, contributing a series to the old *Derbyshire Advertiser* under the title *County Curiosities*. This ran for five years and in response to readers' requests published in book form as *Curiosities of the Peak District*. A third reprint, revised and enlarged to 168 subjects, is now published by Derbyshire Countryside Ltd. under the title *Curiosities of Derbyshire and the Peak District*. For over 50 years he has walked the hills and dales with his wife Dorothy and later their two sons, and is co-author of several books on walking in Derbyshire. For 10 years he has contributed a series of walks to *Derbyshire Life and Countryside*, 31 of which were subsequently published in a book *The Peak District on Foot* which is still available.

He has written and illustrated many articles for the national press, and his pictorial photographs have appeared in the old *Manchester Guardian, Yorkshire Post* and *Staffordshire Advertiser* etc. They have been used on the cover of *Country Life, The Field* and *The Lady,* in guide books and calendars, while several photographs from *Derby Old and New* have appeared on BBC television. In 1994 *Frank Rodgers' Derbyshire* was published with nearly 300 photographs covering the years from 1939 to 1994.

He co-operates with his friend Roy Christian, illustrating his books and articles, and their contributions to *Derbyshire Life and Countryside* extend over many years. Frank's first photograph to appear on the magazine's pages was over 55 years ago, since when he has been a regular contributor.

Contents

Midland Road Railway Station

c. 1840

The first train arrived in Derby in May 1839 and later the decision of the Midland Counties, the Birmingham and Derby Junction and the North Midland Railways to make Derby their centre was of great importance to the town. The station was built in 1840 and was designed by Francis Thompson who also designed several smaller stations in the county. Called the Great Central it stood well out of town at that time, and as can be seen cattle were also transported.

c. 1984

In 1892 the station was altered to the design seen here. This photograph was taken just before demolition was due to begin, British Rail having decided to replace it with a modern station. This decision was made against fierce opposition as the area around it was being restored and conserved by the Historic Buildings Trust as an important part of Derby's railway history.

London Road near the Infirmary - c. 1904

London Road Methodist Chapel of 1861 stands across the road from the Derbyshire Royal Infirmary. The attractive little Cosy Cinema built in 1913 stands on the right and just seen on the nearside left is the Leviathan Hotel. The church in the distance is Holy Trinity. This photograph is undated, but cannot be earlier than 1904 when the first electric tram in Derby ran on this route.

Midland Road Railway Station - 1996

The new station was built despite the opposition. Work began in 1985 and continued through to 1988 when this exterior was completed. Today it stands as an incongruous centrepiece in an area of significant Victorian buildings. The clock pediment with the colourful Midland Railway badge of the Wyvern from the previous station front is now located nearby.

London Road near the Infirmary - 1996

The trams have gone together with the trolley buses which followed, and now diesel buses serve this route. The Cosy Cinema has been converted into the Ristorante La Scala and the hotel has been sacrificed for road widening. The chapel has a modern frontage and been renamed The Queen's Hall, and the plane trees with nearly a century's extra growth now obscure Holy Trinity Church.

Derbyshire Royal Infirmary - 1891

Queen Victoria laid the foundation stone of the Infirmary on London Road in 1891 on the site of the old infirmary of 1810, and one can be fairly sure this photograph was taken soon after its completion. In 1906 a statue of Her Majesty was unveiled at The Spot in Derby by King Edward VII.

London Road – Traffic Street - 1905

The Congregational Church, built in 1842, is just seen on the left at the corner of Traffic Street which runs between the church and Frank Porter, the furniture removers. Bradshaw Street joins opposite. The spire of St. Andrew's Church can be seen faintly in the distance, and the trees on the right stand in the grounds of the Derbyshire Royal Infirmary.

Derbyshire Royal Infirmary – 1996

Although impossible to repeat the same view as the old photograph this view includes the right tower of the old building. Extensive rebuilding in recent years includes this new frontage completed in 1972. Queen Victoria's statue now fronts London Road in the Infirmary grounds.

London Road – Traffic Street – 1996

The Congregational Church was demolished in 1961 after a spell as the Coliseum Cinema. Bradshaw Street, now renamed Bradshaw Way, together with Traffic Street are now dual-carriageways and form a section of the Inner Ring Road. There is a large island at these crossroads and modern additions to the Infirmary are just seen among the trees on the right.

Boden's Lace Mill - 1970

Castlefield's Mill in Castle Street is seen from London Road near the junction with Traffic Street seen on the previous page. This lace mill was built early in the 18th century on the area of Castlefields by Henry Boden, a temperance worker and model employer who provided every amenity for his workers except, of course, alcohol. Well respected as a 'public spirited townsman', Henry Boden lived at The Friary in Friar Gate.

St Peter's Street from the Spot - 1905

Here London Road and Osmaston Road converge with the Babington Lane junction on the left. An electric tramcar is emerging from St. Peter's Street and behind it can be seen the Midland Drapery at the corner of East Street. The sign of a large magnet on this building was a prominent feature of the street. The horse-drawn bread van stands outside Stevenson's, Hatters.

Boden's Lace Mill (site) - 1996

There is now no trace of the mill nor of Castle Street, the area of Castlefields being cleared for the building of the Main Centre seen here and the Eagle Centre which opened later in 1975. Henry Boden is remembered, however, by a plaque on an ornamental piece of ironwork in Bold Lane, all that is left of a small recreation area given by his widow when Henry died in 1908.

St Peter's Street from the Spot - 1996

Window shades are now a thing of the past and shop frontages have been modernised, the Midland Drapery disappearing completely giving a view of the Cathedral tower. Below Babington Lane junction St. Peter's Street is pedestrianised, and this continues up to The Spot on one side, traffic on the left turning in and out of Babington Lane.

Babington Lane from St Peter's Street - 1925

On the left is the canopied entrance to the Grand Theatre of 1886 where many famous people appeared, including Sybil Thorndike and Ivor Novello, the latter playing in *The Rat* in the year this photograph was taken. Beyond the wall at the corner of Gower Street, can be seen the curved north lights of the School of Art built in Green Lane in 1876.

Babington Lane towards St Peter's Street - 1925

Just beyond the tramstop on the left is Gower Street, and beyond that the very popular Picture House. Originally built as the Midland Electric Theatre it was Derby's first cinema, and here one could have tea and cakes while waiting for the next house to begin. When this cosy little cinema closed in the 1960s it had been renamed The Ritz.

Babington Lane from St Peter's Street - 1996

The Grand Theatre building is now Eclipse Nightclub. The modern shops opposite, which include Hunters the furnishers, were erected in the 1920s, Brentfords on the right being built later. In a new one-way system traffic from St. Peter's Street turns into Gower Street together with that from Babington Lane, but is banned from proceeding up Babington Lane from this point.

Babington Lane toward's St Peter's Street - 1996

Modern buildings have transformed the scene, the only buildings remaining from 1925 being those beyond the site of the cinema at the corner of St. Peter's Street. New modern buildings on the right at the corner of Sitwell Street house an electrical and lighting shop called After Dark. Traffic is only allowed down Babington Lane and must turn into Gower Street.

Babington Lane from Burton Road - 1925

This grim block of houses with front doors and few windows was called Malthouse Row and stood on the east side of Babington Lane near its junction with Normanton Road, Burton Road and Green Lane. The town was a great exporter of malt and famous for its brewing, but I could find no record of a malthouse in this area.

Shops in St Peter's Street - c.1860

A fascinating Victorian frontage on the east side of St. Peter's Street below East Street. Note the gas lamp carried on ornamental ironwork, also the Royal Warrant over Kirby's basket shop on the immediate right. Kirby's introduced several unusual items, including a wicker coffin! These shops were demolished about 1882 and replaced by the Midland Drapery.

Babington Lane from Burton Road - 1996

althouse Row was demolished about 1934 and the lane widened into an impressive street. Modern shops now extend from Sitwell Street where there is a large office block, up to this petrol station and car park. There has been no further development since the first issue of this book over twenty years ago.

Shops in St Peter's Street - 1996

he Midland Drapery was demolished and replaced by the present shops opened in 1974. This modern brick architecture is in stark contrast to the impressive stone building which preceded it, and also the Victorian frontage before that. Since the last revision of this book in 1989 the centre of Derby has been transformed by pedestrianisation where folk move freely and unhindered.

St Peter's Street & East Street Corner - 1882

Just showing on the left is St. Peter's Church on the corner of St. Peter's Churchyard with East Street opposite. The Victorian shops have gone to make way for the Midland Drapery, but a memory of those times remains with the horse collars hanging beneath the wall lamp on the left, together with a barber's pole!

Derby School - 1948

Derby School in the churchyard of St. Peter's is seen from St. Peter's Street. It dates from 1554, when Queen Mary included a Free Grammar School among the services to be maintained here by large grants to the town. The pupils who probably brought most honour to the town were John Flamsteed, who became the first Astronomer Royal and Joseph Wright, the famous painter.

St Peter's Street & East Street Corner - 1996

The transition from the scene opposite covers over a century during which time the Midland Drapery has come and gone. The street has passed through the periods of the stage coach, horse and electric tram, trolley and diesel buses, and now all traffic is banned with the pedestrianisation, together with East Street and the entrance to St. Peter's Churchyard.

Derby School - 1996

Today Derby School is completely hidden from St. Peter's Street by an extension to the church. This historic building of old Derby is no longer seen by pedestrians here, who, unhindered by traffic, would now be more able to appreciate it. Today the old school houses The Heritage Centre entered from St. Peter's Churchyard.

East Street - 1885

The Church of St. Peter is seen in the distance at the corner of St. Peter's Street and St. Peter's Churchyard. The Plumber's Arms on the right has closed, waiting to be cleared for road widening. East Street was formerly called Bag Lane, thought to be a corruption of 'burgh' or Saxon earthwork, for this street formed a boundary of the castle which stood nearby.

St Peter's Churchyard - c.1880

Pleasant cottages with flowers on the window sills, stood in this street so near the town centre, although shops are beginning to encroach from St. Peter's Steet down on the right.

East Street - 1996

East Street is now an attractive paved area with seats and trees which extends through from St. Peter's Street to the Morledge, and it was impossible to repeat the view opposite. Even the view taken for the 1989 issue was not possible due to the extra growth of the trees, but this view of St. Peter's Church identifies the scene with the old one.

St Peter's Churchyard - 1996

All the old buildings disappeared many years ago and the takeover by shops is complete. After a period as a very busy street, St. Peter's Churchyard is closed to traffic as seen here at its junction with St. Peter's Street. There is access for traffic from Green Lane only to this point near the church. The Heritage Centre entrance is on the right.

St Peter's Street towards the Cornmarket - c.1880

St. Peter's Street turns left to Victoria Street, and in front of Briggs George and George, the medieval Thorntree Lane joins from the right. Approximately where the cab stands there once stood the town gaol on the bank of the open Markeaton Brook. The brook was crossed by Gaol Bridge, later called St. Peter's Bridge when the gaol was demolished.

Victoria Street from St Peter's Street - 1895

Victoria Street commemorates the coronation of Queen Victoria in 1837. In that year the Markeaton Brook which ran openly down Brookside was culverted and the new street created. The impressive stone buildings of the Royal Hotel and the Athenaeum were built two years later and the Congregational Church replaced the old Brookside Chapel.

St Peter's Street towards the Cornmarket - 1996

The Cornmarket is now paved with a large wrought iron feature at this end. The premises of Briggs George and George have gone revealing H. Samuel at the corner of Albert Street. Here traffic is banned from St. Peter's Street, but a through route still operates along Albert Street and Victoria Street. Thorntree Lane emerges between the Midland Bank and Marks and Spencer.

Victoria Street from St Peter's Street - 1996

Shops now occupy the stone buildings, and in the distance those beside the church have been demolished for the building of Debenhams in 1968. The church too disappeared to be replaced by a modern one on the same site. Reduced traffic now makes the street a much quieter place.

Green Lane - c.1925

This steep street, once called Newlands Lane, at its junction with Victoria Street. The Queen's Head public house, next to the corner on the right, has a small iron plaque recording the height of 4 feet 8 inches in a flood of 1842. On April 1st of that year the townsfolk awoke to find the Markeaton Brook, which entered the culvert beneath St. James Bridge seen on page 22, had flooded in the night.

Victoria Street towards St Peter's Street - c.1880

Athenaeum and Royal Hotel on the left face Green Lane, and in the centre distance the building of Briggs George and George stands at the junction of St. Peter's Street. The diminutive building on the left houses the Derbyshire Building Society who later moved to the large building at the corner of Green Lane.

The Queen's Head and a long line of buildings which included the well-known Ranby's store, were demolished in 1962 to be replaced by Debenhams. Once a very busy corner, this end of Green Lane was closed to traffic, except for deliveries, in 1973. The flood plaque is now fixed beside this entrance to Debenhams.

Victoria Street towards St Peter's Street - 1996

There is little change on the left, but Briggs George and George in the centre distance has been replaced by the Midland Bank. The corner of Debenhams just shows on the right, but beyond Green Lane the smaller buildings have been replaced by more imposing ones. The Derbyshire Building Society is now situated in imposing premises in the Market Place.

Victoria Street & St James Lane - 1866

The narrow St. James Lane on the right joins Victoria Street at St. James Bridge. Here Markeaton Brook entered the culvert built in 1837 along Brookside, now Victoria Street. The notice in St. James Lane reads 'L. Smitherd, Chimney Sweeper and Fire Extinguisher' and those on the right 'J. Eagers, Working Cutler and Grinder' and 'R. Johnson, Lock and Whitesmith'.

Becket Street - c.1875

When Becket Street was built in the 1820s the fine Jacobean House in the Wardwick, seen on the right, was cut through and part of it 'turned into' Becket Street. With the date over the door, 1677, it is claimed as the first brick house to be built in the town, with two acres of ornamental gardens beyond the wall seen on the right. The Cathedral tower is seen across the Wardwick.

Victoria Street & St James Street - 1996

In 1878 the covering of the brook was continued to Sadler Gate Bridge at the bottom end of Sadler Gate, creating a new street, The Strand. St. James Lane was widened and renamed St. James Street and in 1869 the G.P.O. occupied the building on the right. Traffic from Victoria Street can proceed along The Wardwick to the left and The Strand, but deliveries only enter St. James Street.

Becket Street - 1996

New buildings in 1974 took the last small portion of the remaining gardens of the Jacobean House, and ahead the Museum and Art Gallery in the Wardwick obscures the Cathedral tower except for the tips of the pinnacles. Traffic flows both ways in Becket Street, but can only turn left into the Wardwick.

Friar Gate - c.1875

The Old White Horse Inn, together with several thatched cottages, are thought to have stood in Friar Gate since before 1751. They were due for demolition when this photograph was taken to make way for the bridge carrying the Great Northern Railway. Before the Black Friars established their Friary here in 1792, Friar Gate was known as Markeaton Lane.

Public Transport - 1907

Horse-drawn trams, introduced in 1880, were taken over by the Corporation in 1899 and ended with the one shown here in November 1907. Before 1880 horse-drawn buses were run privately and continued to run until 1915. This posed photograph shows a policeman with the conductor, an official in the foreground and another official with the driver.

Friar Gate - 1996

The ornate cast-iron railway bridge was erected in 1878, and is the work of a famous engineering firm Andrew Handyside which closed down in 1911. The line is now defunct and the future of the bridge in doubt as it lies on the proposed route of the inner ring road. It has been declared an object of historical importance and Friar Gate a Conservation Area.

Public Transport - 1996

Electric trams started in 1904 to be superseded by trolley buses in 1932, the conversion taking three years. Since 1967 Derby has been served by motor buses, and today single and double-deck City Riders operate. During the almost ninety years since the old photograph was taken and the various forms of transport that have passed this spot, the building has remained a chemists.

George Yard - 1900

Often passed unnoticed, George Yard is entered beneath an arch at the bottom end of Sadler Gate. It ran parallel with that street to the George Inn in Iron Gate. Although an inn yard it is typical of several medieval streets in the town such as Thorntree Lane. Before the building of the theatre in 1773 in Bold Lane nearby, a room in George Yard was used by actors.

The Strand towards Cheapside - 1920

The culverting of Markeaton Brook creating The Strand (see page 23) ended at Sadler Gate Bridge, one of ten bridges over the brook in the town. Some years ago it was revealed when a steam-roller crashed through the culvert. Wallaces has the long windows of a 'stockingers house' overlooking trees in Boden's Pleasaunce (see page 9). On the immediate left are the Library buildings and cottages.

George Yard - 1996

S ome of the old buildings have gone, but the scene can be identified by the stone sets of the road and pavement and the tower of the Cathedral almost hidden by a modern block of offices. The road now loops round to rejoin Sadler Gate opposite the Bell Inn.

The Strand towards Cheapside - 1996

T he Wallace building is now undergoing changes, and Boden's Pleasaunce has been sacrificed for Bold Lane car park, seen in the distance, but the ironwork feature has been retained. The old cottages have been replaced by an extension to the Library of a Reference Library and Museum and incorporating a Museum shop, built in 1966.

Jury Street - c.1900

Bold Lane continues as Jury Street, or Jewry Street. It here meets Willow Row seen on the left beyond the Bird Inn in an area of mean courtyards. Walker Lane comes down on the right from Queen Street.

Queen Street towards Iron Gate - c.1912

The tower of All Saints' Church is seen faintly behind the lamp standard, with the Dolphin Inn just showing beyond the edge of the Nottingham Castle on the immediate left. This stands at the junction of St. Michael's Lane. On the right further down emerges Walker Lane where the 'walkers' lived who were employed treading the fuller's earth in the fulling mills in Full Street opposite.

The Bird Inn was demolished about 1909 and later the whole area was cleared, nothing remaining to identify the scene today. Jury Street now sweeps right into Walker Lane and on to join the inner ring road as part of the one-way system leading north out of the city. It was opened in 1970, while Willow Row loops back to Walker Lane along Cathedral Road.

Queen Street towards Iron Gate - 1996

The tower of All Saints' Church, now the Cathedral, is prominent and together with the row of buildings and the Dolphin Inn comprise one of the city's most pleasing groups. The demolition of the Nottingham Castle reveals a glimpse of St. Michael's Church. All the buildings on the right were demolished in 1925 and Walker Lane widened and renamed Cathedral Road.

Queen Street towards King Street - 1882

When St. Alkmund's Church was built in 1846 it almost obscured St. Mary's R.C. Church except for the edges of its tower just seen down the sides of St. Alkmund's. It was felt that St. Mary's, built by Pugin in 1838-39, had been deliberately hidden from Queen Street, and for a long time St. Alkmund's spire was referred to as St. Alkmund's spite! The Nottingham Castle in St. Michael's Lane had good stabling and J.H. Frost advertised his Smithy at Castle Forge. A notice below these informs us that a timber mill sells English and Foreign timber. In the distance Queen Street seems blocked by the churchyard of St. Alkmund's, and here it turns left into King Street.

King Street Methodist Church - c.1965

This Methodist Church in King Street, only a stone's throw from St. Alkmund's was described by Sir Nikolaus Pevsner as having 'a fine stately Grecian front, a one-storeyed Greek Doric porch and an upper floor with Ionic pilasters'. Replacing a chapel of 1805, it was built in 1841 at a cost of £5,000 and accommodated about 1,600 people with a school room below for 500 children.

Queen Street towards King Street - 1996

St. Mary's Church now dominates the scene from Queen Street, for in 1967-68 St. Alkmund's was demolished to make way for the Inner Ring Road, St. Alkmund's Way. The buildings left and right have gone except for St. Michael's which closed in 1977 but is now occupied by the architects, Derek Latham & Co. Ltd. On the left is seen the firm of John Smith, the famous clockmakers.

King Street Methodist Church - 1996

The church was demolished at the same time as St. Alkmund's to clear the way for the inner ring road. It was replaced by a multi-storey car park in 1971 which has its entrance in Chapel Street seen on the left, while its modern style is seen from the ring road on page 35.

St Mary's Roman Catholic Church - c.1915

St. Mary's is seen from the west doorway of St. Alkmund's in St. Alkmund's Churchyard with Bridge Gate beyond the iron bollards. Houses fronted a paved way around three sides of St. Alkmund's, and in his series *The Buildings of England* Sir Nikolaus Pevsner calls St. Alkmund's Church Yard 'a revival of 18th century unmatched, a quiet oasis'.

An Ancient Crossing - 1900

The second entrance to St. Alkmund's Churchyard from Bridge Gate. To quote Pevsner again 'no houses are specially noteworthy but the ensemble is very satisfying'. This is one of the town's oldest crossings where Bridge Gate is crossed by Darley Lane from where this sketch was made. Many packhorses laden with lead from the Derbyshire hills must have passed this way, probably the oldest route into the town from the north. A pinnacle of All Saints' Church can just be seen over the chancel of St. Alkmund's.

St Mary's Roman Catholic Church - 1996

The quiet oasis has been swept away together with St. Alkmund's Church, the Inner Ring Road of St. Alkmund's Way cutting deeply where it once stood. This photograph, taken from the same spot as the one opposite, shows a footbridge which crosses to St. Mary's Church.

An Ancient Crossing (site) - 1996

A crossing no longer, the junction with Bridge Gate disappearing when that street was replaced by the Inner Ring Road, the only link with the sketch opposite being the tower of the Cathedral. St. Alkmund's Church has gone, and among the trees seen on the right there remains a small portion of its wall. In a low arch a tablet records that 'foundations of successive buildings from the 8th century' were uncovered when the church was demolished, and a further discovery was a sarcophagus carved with interlaced work and believed to be that of St. Alkmund which now rests in the Museum.

St Alkmund's Church - 1930

Here Bridge Gate passes St. Alkmund's Church after climbing from St. Mary's Bridge. Beside the overhanging gable on the left is seen an entrance to St. Alkmund's Churchyard seen on page 32. Bridge Gate was probably the oldest east to west crossing in the town.

View from St. Mary's Bridge - 1948

View from St. Mary's Bridge, looking up Bridge Gate to the churches of St. Alkmund's and St. Mary's. On the left is the 14th century chapel of St. Mary's on the Bridge which stands on the two remaining arches of the previous bridge of 1300, the present bridge being built beside it in 1794. One of only a handful of bridge chapels still standing in this country, it is Derby's finest antiquity.

St Alkmund's Church (site) - 1996

Nothing remains to identify this scene with the one opposite, the far lane of St. Alkmund's Way running about twenty feet directly beneath the site of the church. The portion of wall mentioned on page 33 is hidden high on the bank on the left and is the base of the far side of the church. The footbridge crosses to St. Mary's Church, and beyond is the bridge carrying King Street, a slip road comes down from it on the right. A glimpse of Chapel Street Car Park is seen on the left.

View from St. Mary's Bridge - 1996

Bridge Gate and St. Alkmund's Church were sacrificed when the inner ring road of St. Alkmund's Way was built. The bridge over this once important river crossing now carries secondary traffic to and from the city centre, passing underneath the inner ring road just visible on the left. A footpath bordered by new houses climbs to St. Mary's Church.

The Derwent from St Mary's Bridge - c.1940

This conglomeration of buildings includes the old Silk Mill, the Power Station of the 1920s and the Cathedral. An ancient causeway, perhaps large stepping stones, once crossed the river on approximately the line of the low weir which diverted water to the Silk Mill. On the left can be seen the rounded clock tower of the old Town Hall.

Silk Mill Lane - 1920

One of the town's historic spots, for England's first silk mill was erected here in 1717. John Crochet had built a mill here in 1702 and this was extended by John Lombe who installed Italian type machinery and turned it into the 'first factory in the modern sense'. To quote one statistic - '73,726 yards of silk were made at every turn of the water wheel'. The mill was almost destroyed by fire and rebuilt, the portion seen here looking very similar to the original. The tower housed a bell which called the operators to work. The splendid wrought-iron gates, entrance to the mill, stand on a bridge over the mill stream, and were the work of Robert Bakewell, the town's fine craftsman of the 17th century.

The Derwent from St Mary's Bridge - 1996

A modern concrete span, Causey Bridge, carries St. Alkmund's Way across the river on roughly the line of the old causeway. Several of the old buildings have gone which, together with the demolition of the Power Station in 1971 is a great improvement, although the East Midlands Electricity Board has generators housed in modern buildings there.

Silk Mill Lane - 1996

The workmen's cottages have gone and been replaced by modern buildings which house generators of the Electricity Board. The Silk Mill was opened in 1974 as the Industrial Museum, and Robert Bakewell's gates which had stood for many years in the Wardwick have been erected between the Mill tower and the modern buildings, a few yards from their original position.

Full Street Junction & Queen Street - 1920

A very narrow Full Street here joins an equally narrow Queen Street. The Dolphin Inn, which has stood here since the 16th century and faces into Queen Street, is seen on the left corner.

All Saints Parish Church - 1882

The church of All Saints, seen from Full Street at the junction with Amen Alley which runs beside the churchyard to Iron Gate. The overhanging house was once a shop which sold religious books. Behind where the photographer stood were the Devonshire Almshouses built by the famous Bess of Hardwick, Countess of Shrewsbury and ancestor of the Cavendishes whose ornate monument stands in the church. Designed by herself and built in her own lifetime, it carries the information, in Latin, of her four husbands and great houses including Chatsworth. It is said that she often came here to gaze on this monument. Here too was buried John Lombe, of Silk Mill fame with a splendid funeral in 1722. He was only 29, and according to legend his early demise was from poison administered by an Italian woman in revenge for his having stolen the secrets of silk throwing on a visit to Italy.

Full Street Junction & Queen Street - 1996

Only the Dolphin Inn can be recognised from the view opposite, the buildings in front being demolished in 1925, together with those on the right revealing Walker Lane, then widened and renamed Cathedral Road. The Queen Street baths on the right were built in 1932. This corner is now controlled by traffic lights with one-way traffic in Full Street entering from this end.

The Cathedral - 1996

In 1927 All Saints' Church became the Cathedral, and in 1968 was extended as seen here. The tower dates from the early 16th century and is considered a fine example of the Perpendicular style. At a height of 178 feet it is second only to Boston Stump among our parish church towers. An almost illegible inscription 'Young Men and Maidens' carved on the tower seems to support the tradition that it was partly paid for by the young people of the town when built in 1523. Other contributions came from the sale of 'church ales' at village wakes, a not uncommon practice at that time.

Full Street - c.1920

The houses on the right had gardens down to the Derwent. A cab stands outside the entrance to the Devonshire Almshouses mentioned on page 38 and behind the cab is seen the wall of All Saints Churchyard.

Derwent Street - c.1935

This photograph may have been taken about 1935 as trolley buses came in in 1932 and the buildings on the right were demolished in 1938 for the building of the Council House. Exeter Bridge built in 1929 over the River Derwent, can be seen in the distance, and beyond that the Derwent Foundry. The ground on the left has been cleared for the building of the new Police Headquarters.

With the building of the extension in 1968, the church, now the Cathedral, extends to the road. All the houses on the right have gone, the ground now landscaped down to the river. In 1995 the statue of Prince Charles Stuart, Bonnie Prince Charlie, seen on the right, was erected to commemorate his arrival and retreat here in his abortive attempt to take the throne in 1745.

Derwent Street - 1996

In 1939-41 the Council House replaced the old buildings, and a decorative island now stands at the intersection of Full Street and Corporation Street with Derwent Street, the last one no longer continuing into the Market Place. The banks of the river are attractive gardens with riverside walks reached by steps beside the bridge.

The Derwent from Exeter Bridge - c.1955

This photograph of the view upstream from Exeter Bridge about 40 years ago shows a very industrialised River Derwent. The Power Station on the left was built in 1922, and among the buildings on the right are Smart and Elsoms, timber merchants. The old Silk Mill together with Sowter's Flour Mill are central to the scene.

Rotton Row - 1860

Ahead is Iron Gate with Sadler Gate on the left and Market Head opposite. On the right is a large detached block filling the west side of the Market Place comprising The Shambles (butchers) and a colonnaded walk on two sides called the Piazzas. As the main route north and south through the town, Rotton Row is a corruption of the Norman 'Route du Roi' or King's Highway.

The Derwent from Exeter Bridge - 1996

The Power Station was demolished in 1971 and the ground landscaped down to the river with open ground from the bridge to the Silk Mill. This is the only sign of industry remaining in the scene and a worthy home for the Industrial Museum. The unsightly collection on the right has been replaced by the Family Health Service. This pleasant river scene is enhanced by trees.

Rotton Row (now the Market Place) - 1996

The large block of buildings has gone, Rotton Row and Market Head are now part of the Market Place. The whole area is paved. Prominent in the scene is a curved waterfall, built in 1995, which has caused much adverse comment. The Derbyshire Building Society is seen behind on the Iron Gate corner.

Market Place towards Iron Gate - 1869

The Shambles and Piazzas fill the view towards Iron Gate and Sadler Gate. When they were demolished in 1871 there was much jollification with fireworks and a band. The stone-paved Market Place, used for many purposes including a parade ground, was thus enlarged to its present size. Note the 'Music Warehouse' sign on the left.

Iron Gate from Sadler Gate - 1866

It is hard to imagine that Iron Gate was a continuation of the King's Highway, one of the most important routes through the town. It curved past All Saints' Church seen faintly in the distance and then passed St. Alkmund's to continue along Darley Lane on its way northwards. The three top-hatted policemen stand outside The George, an ancient coaching inn at the top of George Yard. The white cornered building on the left stands on the corner of Sadler Gate and houses the famous printing firm of Bemrose. Iron Gate was widened the year after this photograph was taken, and it is possible the right side was due for demolition.

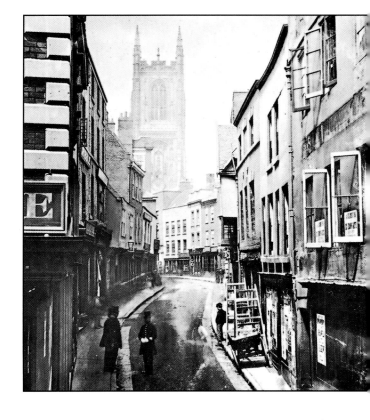

Market Place towards Iron Gate - 1996

In the last revision of this book in 1989 the War Memorial filled the view. In the new landscaping of the Market Place the War Memorial was moved and today the view is filled with trees and attractive walkways. Iron Gate runs to the left of the Derbyshire Building Society.

Iron Gate from Sadler Gate - 1996

The widening of the street in 1867 entailed the rebuilding of the right side. Bemrose's building on the left is now Lloyds Bank and the George Inn still stands today. Beyond these are Foulds' music shop, Flint, Bishop and Barnett, solicitors, and Ladbrokes, the bookmakers. The street is paved as far as All Saints', now the Cathedral, and on the wide pavement on the left stands the Joseph Wright obelisk shown on page 47.

Iron Gate towards the Market Place - 1860

I ron Gate curves left to the Market Place with the junction of Sadler Gate seen on the right. Some indication of the street name is shown here, for it is the street of the blacksmiths. The word 'gate' means 'way', and comes from the time of the Danish occupation. On the right, close by where the photographer stood, was the house where the famous artist, Joseph Wright, 'Wright of Derby' was born in 1730. When Prince Charles Stuart reached Derby in his invasion of 1745, the Wright family, like many others, had moved out of the town for safety. Upon returning after Prince Charles' retreat they found their house had been a billet for no less than 43 soldiers!

Market Place and Town Hall - c.1900

A busy day in the Market Place nearly 100 years ago. A market had been held here since the 13th century and there have been four Town Halls, the present one erected in 1842 after the destruction by fire of the previous building of 1828. The statue of Sir Thomas Bass, who was a great benefactor to the town, was unveiled in 1885. Note the horse-drawn trams and carriages in a scene full of interest.

Iron Gate towards the Market Place - 1996

Widened by the demolition of the left side and the paving of the street, Iron Gate takes on a new look, the view now extending through the Market Place into the Cornmarket. The birthplace of Joseph Wright is recorded on the stone obelisk seen here, erected in 1992. It is surmounted by an abstract feature of perhaps his finest work 'The Orrery' which hangs in the Art Gallery.

Market Place and Guildhall - 1996

The Market Place has witnessed many events, from public whippings to celebrations. The Town Hall is now the Guildhall, and the *Derbyshire Advertiser* which was here from 1880 to 1969 has gone, the building, originally the Cross Keys Inn, now classed of historic interest. The markets have moved to new sites while the statue now stands in Museum Square in the Wardwick.

Assembly Rooms - c.1943

For well over two centuries the Assembly Rooms graced Derby Market Place. Built in the 1700s by Joseph Pickford, they were designed by Washington Shirley, 5th Earl Ferrers of Staunton Harold near Melbourne. The huge tympanum depicting musical instruments was by the Nottingham carver Ratcliffe, and the interior, the scene of many important social events, was by Robert Adam. Taken during the last war, this photograph shows a large 'thermometer' which recorded the changing National War Savings total.

St James Lane - 1870

St. James Lane seen here from the Cornmarket, took its name from the Cluniac monastery of 1140 which stood nearby. Together with George Yard and Thorntree Lane it is typical of the narrow streets of medieval times. The interest of the onlookers shows that the camera was not so commonplace as it is today.

Assembly Rooms - 1996

Following a fire in 1963 the main building was demolished but the façade was saved and re-erected at the entrance to the National Tramway Museum at Crich. A splendid chandelier from the rooms now hangs in the Council House Reception Suite. Today the Tourist Information Centre stands on the site of the old building with the new Assembly Rooms above and to the left.

St James Street - 1996

The new status of 'street' came about when St. James Lane was widened. Barclays Bank, St. James Restaurant (Jimmy's) and a number of building societies are among the establishments here. Only delivery traffic can now enter from Victoria Street, the Cornmarket end having been paved.

Mayor's Parlour - 1947

The Mayor's Parlour stood in a yard off Tenant Street, and the opportunity was taken to photograph it just before demolition in 1948. Once a private residence, history does not record any evidence of a connection with the Mayor either as a home or as offices!

Tenant Street - 1977

Although the Mayor's Parlour, which was demolished in 1948 stood only a few yards from these buildings on the corner of Tenant Street and Derwent Street, they stood until 1986. Offices on the corner were variously occupied by local government departments which later became shops, including Philipson's Seed Merchants. In 1931 The Britannic Insurance Co. Ltd. had offices in Morris House on the corner which looked across to the old Assembly Rooms in the Market Place. The DCOD on the shop front indicates the Derby Corporation Omnibus Department restaurant, the wartime Civic Restaurant.

Mayor's Parlour (site) - 1996

In the first edition of this book (1974) the site of the Mayor's Parlour was shown as a grassy plot. In the intervening years the idea for a new library here was abandoned as too was the intention to build a large hotel, this latter after the excavation of a huge hole (the 'infamous hole'). This has now been filled in, and we are back to normal with decorative gardens now gracing the spot.

Tenant Street - 1996

With the demolition of all the buildings on this corner in 1986 an open view across the gardens to the Market Place and new Assembly Rooms is revealed. Tenant Street is closed to traffic, as too is this end of Derwent Street where it enters the Market Place, both being paved.

The Morledge from Tenant Street - c.1930

The parapet of Tenant Street Bridge is seen on the left where the Markeaton Brook emerges to join the River Derwent. When the brook was culverted from St. Peter's Bridge in 1844-45 eight men were killed here when the bridge roof collapsed. Albert Street was created along the line of the culvert. Behind Stewart's Seed Stores can be seen the base of the Shot Tower.

The Fish Market - 1980

The Market Hall, situated behind the Town Hall and extending through to Albert Street, was built at a cost of £29,000, and opened with great ceremony in 1866. In 1926 this fine southern aspect in Albert Street was spoiled by the addition of the Fish, Game and Poultry Market.

The Morledge from Tenant Street - 1996

Tenant Street Bridge has gone, the culvert now extending to the river beneath the River Gardens. The Morledge is now a dual carriageway and Cockpit Hill has been replaced by the market stall area of the Eagle Centre. These market stalls were transferred from covered stalls built in 1933 to house the open stalls of the Morledge. The Derby Combined Court Centre now stands on this site.

The Fish Market (site) - 1996

The Fish Market, as it was popularly called, was demolished in 1981 and its activities transferred to Lockup Yard off the Cornmarket. Uncle Tom's snack bar was retained and attractive shops now stand on the left side. With the twinning of Derby and Osnabruck the area was named Osnabruck Square in 1985, and a carved stone column informs us that the German city is 500 miles away.

The Morledge - 1931

A non-market day gives little indication of the bustle and activity which has taken place here through the centuries. The towers of All Saints' Church and the Town Hall are prominent, while the Shot Tower has dominated the scene from 1808. Molten lead was poured through a sieve at the top of the tower, the drops becoming spherical as they fell.

Morledge Market - 1964

The Morledge Market was built in 1933, and housed the open stalls from the Morledge, mentioned above, and although covered, retained the open atmosphere. A busy Saturday afternoon in 1964 is seen here, with a policeman controlling pedestrians over a crossing near the Bus Station.

The Morledge - 1996

This view is identified by the Cathedral tower and the dome of the Guildhall, together with a few unchanged buildings on the far left. On the right stands the Derby Combined Court Centre opened in 1989. The open stalls seen in the old photograph opposite were re-housed on this site with permanent covers before being removed to the Eagle Centre just visible on the left.

Morledge Market (site) - 1996

The market moved to the Eagle Centre in 1975 and the new Combined Court Centre built on the site. Gardens extending down to the river have been retained.

Cockpit Hill - 1930

This slight mound in the Morledge was the site of the castle of which little is known. Formerly Castle Hill, it became Cockpit Hill when the barbaric pastime of cockfighting took place there. It continued as an open market until the site was cleared in the development of the Eagle Centre. The Canal Tavern - with 'Good Stabling' - indicates the nearness of the canal.

Morledge from Cockpit Hill - c.1930

The Morledge widens towards Cattle Market Road where the road crosses the canal at Cattle Market Bridge seen in the distance. The Cattle Market has stood beside the river here since 1861.

Opened in 1975 by Sir Derek Ezra MBE (now Lord Ezra), the Eagle Centre is an extensive area of shops, large stores and the once open market in the Morledge. The footbridge crosses over to the Bus Station, and behind is the market stall area of the Centre. This frontage to the Centre has been completely re-designed since the last issue of this book in 1989.

Morledge from the former Cockpit Hill - 1996

Cattle Market Bridge and the canal have disappeared without trace, while the Cattle Market was moved over the river in 1970. The Bus Station has replaced the buildings on the left, a footbridge crossing to the Eagle Centre. Traffic from the right and left converge here for the Inner Ring Road seen in the distance where it bears right for the south or crosses the river for the north and east.

The Ice Factory - c.1977

Popularly known as the Ice Factory, this grim building in the Morledge was more correctly called Derby Pure Ice and Cold Storage, and besides selling ice it stored meat, eggs and butter, and, oddly, fur coats. It was built at the turn of the century by Sir Alfred Haslam, the pioneer of refrigeration in ships.

Riverside Scene - 1870

In the early 1700s the Derwent was dredged and straightened and a wharf was constructed, the first boat arriving in 1721. By the end of the century there were foundries, a rolling and slitting mill, lead smelting, and gypsum and plaster works here. Prominent on the left is the Shot Tower and just to its right the dome of the Town Hall. Seen faintly over the river on the right is the tower of All Saints' Church.

The Ice Factory (site) - 1996

With the introduction of the home freezer the demand for ice melted and tenders for the demolition of this four-storey 'Victorian Monstrosity' were invited. This took place soon after the old photograph opposite was taken and the area is now the Cockpit Hill Car Park awaiting development. Beyond the footbridge are seen the roofs of the new court buildings.

Riverside Scene - 1996

Many of the old industries had gone when the site was cleared in 1931 for the building of the Open Market and the Bus Station, and later the Council House. This view across the Bus Station shows the Cathedral tower beyond the Council House and the new court buildings to the left.

Canal Lock near the River - 1905

The opening of the Derby Canal in 1795, connecting the town with the Trent and Mersey Canal at Swarkestone, gave added stimulous to the wharf. Here is Morledge Lock, the canal crossing the river at Long Bridge a short distance to the right. The tower of All Saints' Church, the spire of St. Alkmund's, the tower of St. Mary's and the stubby tower of the Silk Mill can all be picked out on the skyline.

Long Bridge - c.1948

This simple structure carried the towpath of the Derby Canal which crossed the Derwent as mentioned above. Besides the normal cargoes, country folk were conveyed into Derby on Market Days for 6d (2½p), and several tons of coal carried free into the town each week for the benefit of the poor. To the left is seen part of the Cattle Market on The Holmes.

Canal Lock near the River (site) - 1996

No trace of the canal remains, only the tower of the Cathedral showing above the Council House and that of St. Mary's identifying the scene. The Bus Station car park fills the foreground, fronted by the Inner Ring Road.

Long Bridge (site) - 1996

By 1935 the canal was barely operational but the bridge continued to be used by pedestrians. It closed in 1959 as unsafe and was subsequently demolished. The Cattle Market moved over the river in 1970. The land beyond the weir has been landscaped and is crossed by the Inner Ring Road.

The Weir on the Derwent - c.1930

The line of the Derby Canal crossing the river is indicated by the Long Bridge seen above the weir. The Shot Tower is dominant to the scene with the dome of the Corn Exchange in Albert Street on the left. Immediately right of the Shot Tower is seen the long roof of the Market Hall of 1866, and extreme right the clock tower of the Town Hall. Note the spelling of the word 'color'.

Exeter Bridge - c.1905

This fine stone bridge of 1852 replaced a wooden one of about 1810. It takes its name from the Earl of Exeter whose town house stood nearby in Full Street. Prince Charles Stuart stayed here in his march on London in 1745, when the fateful decision was made to retreat. Panelling from the historic room was saved and may be seen in the Bonnie Prince Charlie Room in Derby Museum.

The Weir on the Derwent - 1996

The Council House is seen on the right with the Town Hall (now the Guildhall) clock tower just showing above. The Shot Tower and industrial buildings have gone, replaced by the Court buildings in the Morledge. The road in the foreground is part of the complex forming the Inner Ring Road from which this photograph was taken.

Exeter Bridge - 1996

The old photograph was taken from the Long Bridge shown on the previous two pages. With that now gone, this more distant view clearly shows the changes; the Council House on the left, the concrete bridge of 1929, and the Police Headquarters replacing the corn merchant and bakery. Both banks of the river are laid out in attractive gardens and riverside walks.

The Siddals - 1874

The opening of the Derby Canal was of great benefit to the town, and here at the Siddals, open ground close by the river and just south of the town, are seen the lock gates and lock-keeper's house. Cattle Market Bridge is seen in the distance.

The Siddals - 1996

The canal has disappeared without trace and a new road, Station Approach, has been built on the route of the canal. To the left is a very busy junction where it joins the Inner Ring Road. The cones control the traffic, for a new road is being constructed which crosses the river and continues to a large development project called Pride Park behind the railway station.